This Journal Belongs To:

____

Made in the USA
Columbia, SC
29 November 2023

27365792R00068